ETHAN'S DREAM TRIP TO THE FARM

Written by

Nigel Morris

ETHAN'S DREAM TRIP TO THE FARM

ISBN: 979-8-218-52291-9

written by

Nigel Morris

Illustrations by

Zari Khan.

Book Blurb

Ethan, a smart and kind-hearted boy with sparkling brown eyes, lives in the lively and bustling city of Detroit.
Ethan's life is filled with love for animals, and his wishes are simple—to visit an animal farm and for his parents take him.
Will his wishes ever come true?
Join Ethan on an unforgettable journey as his dreams become reality. When his school organizes a trip to the biggest animal farm in town, Ethan's excitement knows no bounds.
How will he react when he comes face to face with his beloved animals? What lessons will he learn from this adventure?
Amidst feeding ducks and marveling at dairy cattle, Ethan's compassion deepens, leading to a heartfelt decision that will change his life and family forever.
Embark on a story where the simplest wishes bring about the most profound changes.

Ethan was a smart and kind brown-skinned boy with black wavy hair and sparkling brown eyes. He lived in the large and bustling city of Detroit. Ethan lived together with his parents in their small and cozy home. He loved watching documentaries on TV, swimming, skate boarding, and riding his bike with his best friends, Jaxon and Imani.

Ethan loved animals, especially chickens and sheep. He was only fives years old when his parents had taken him along on a visit to their friend's small barn. And he became so fascinated by the way they moved and the sounds they made.

Even then, Ethan's love for these animals grew stronger and he wished mom and dad would own a farm.

"Little man, there's a lot of work that goes into animal farming and mommy and daddy are too busy now," dad had explained as calmly as he could. Ethan was sad but daddy told him they could have one some day.

It was a cool Saturday morning and Ethan was watching a kids show on TV about animals. Suddenly, he wished more than ever to visit one with lot of animals.His imagination ran wild wondering about all the other animals he would

possibly see for the first time. Ethan watched the rest of the show with his wish buried in his heart.

And the most incredible thing happened at school the following Monday!

"Kids, I have good news for you!" Ethan's class teacher Mrs. Julie said with excitement.

"What do you think it is?" Jaxon asked.
"I don't know," Imani replied.
"We will be going to the biggest farm in the city in two weeks!" Mrs. Julie announced.
The kids all froze with excitement!!

"Yay!" the class cheered.
"How is this real?" Ethan whispered, his eyes huge
"Maybe it's about surprise trip," Ethan

"Mom!" Ethan screamed immediately he entered the house.
"What is it, Ethan?" mom asked.
"Guess what! My class will be visiting the biggest animal farm in the city!" Ethan said proudly, he couldn't contain his excitement.
"I'm so happy to hear that, Ethan," mom said "You finally got your wish, honey!"

Mom laughed and said, "I can tell that you are very excited. So when is your trip to the animal farm? Would you like me to go with you?"
"Yes! I can't wait to tell dad!" spoke Ethan from the top of his lungs.
"C'mon, mom! I'm not a kid, and we're all going with the bus!"

Ethan went up to his room and every night, he dreamed about the farm.

Finally, it was the day of the trip and Ethan woke up excited. "Ethan, your bus will arrive soon," mom and dad called from downstairs. "And you need to eat breakfast too," mom added. "Coming, Mom!" Ethan yelled and while getting dressed as fast as he could. Soon he was downstairs having his yummy breakfast of toast, eggs, and bacon with orange juice.

A few minutes later, he was on the bus going to the animal farm!

“Make sure you stick together at all times, and don’t go touching anything, okay?” Mrs. Julie cautioned.
“Yes, Mrs. Julie,” they replied as one.

"Welcome to the animal farm! We are so happy to have you here today, and I am Fletcher," the keeper of the animal farm greeted cheerfully.

"Wow," the kids gasped. The farm was nothing like they imagined. It was huge and they didn't know which way to go first.

"Today, I'll be showing you around the farm. I hope you have a fun

He introduced different animals. There were cattle, sheep, goats, horses, pigs, snakes, ducks, rabbits, turkeys, and even domestic water buffalo! Ethan and his friends were amazed to see these animals in their sheds.

"Wow! look at that!"
Ethan pointed at the
water buffalo.

He paused for a moment and asked Mrs. Julie. “Do water buffalo bite people?”
“Yes, they are very aggressive and dangerous, ” Mrs. Julie replied, “But not these ones, they are gentle Well, unless you scare them.” “Wow,” Jaxon said.

Imani asked the next question. “Can ducks see in the dark?” “Yes, Imani. Unlike chickens, they can’t see in the dark,” Mrs. Julie answered. “Wow! I wish I could be a duck!” said Imani and everyone laughed.

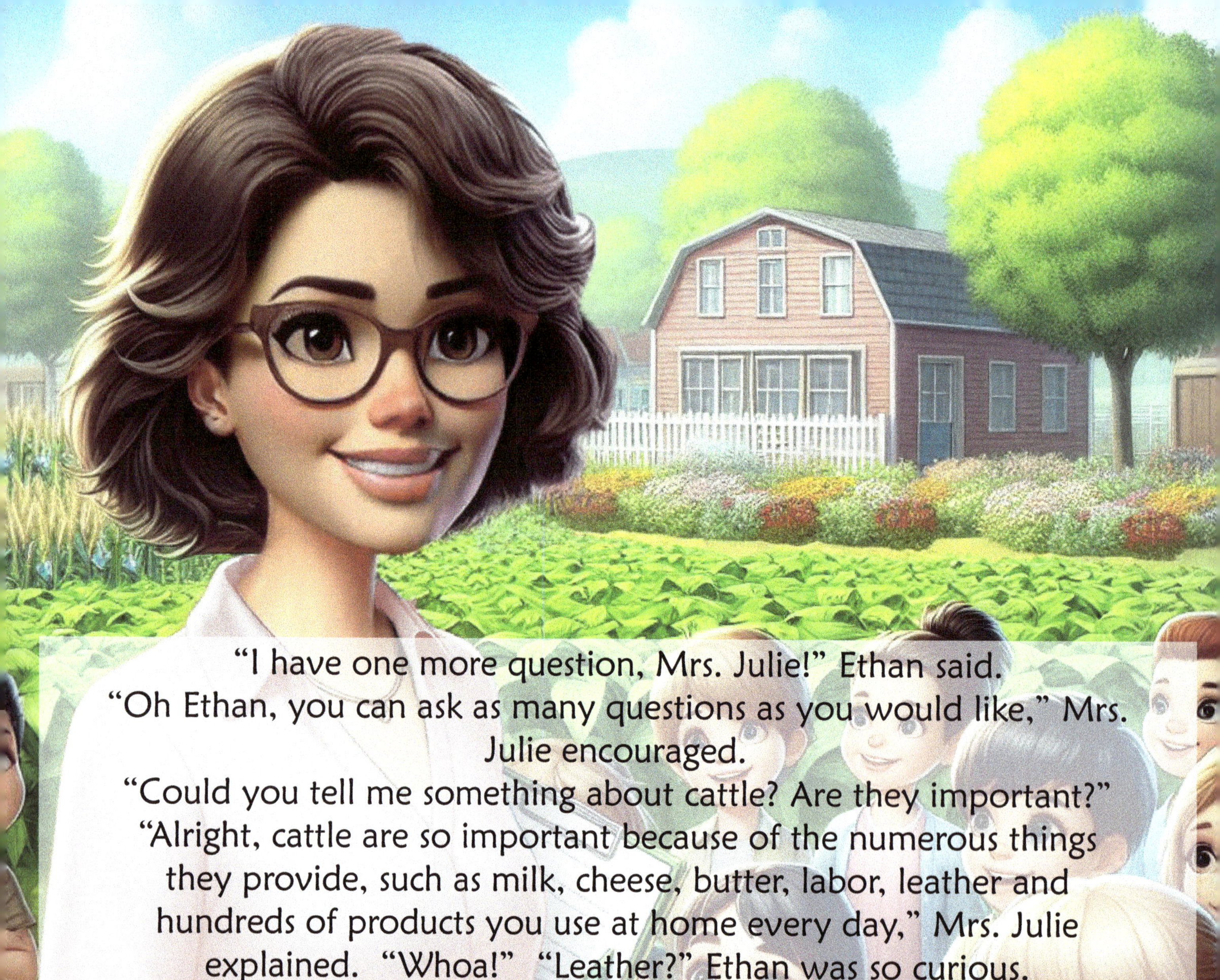

"I have one more question, Mrs. Julie!" Ethan said.
"Oh Ethan, you can ask as many questions as you would like," Mrs. Julie encouraged.
"Could you tell me something about cattle? Are they important?"
"Alright, cattle are so important because of the numerous things they provide, such as milk, cheese, butter, labor, leather and hundreds of products you use at home every day," Mrs. Julie explained. "Whoa!" "Leather?" Ethan was so curious.
"Yes, the skin of cattle serves as leather so most of you are able to wear your shoes, bags and even clothes because of the cattle," Mrs. Julie said. "I didn't know that," someone said. "What did you mean by labor, Mrs. Julie?" another asked.
"Cows are so strong and often pull strong equipment on the farm."

The kids continued asking questions until Mr. Fletcher came around. "C'mon, you guys should see the fun stuff," he said and the followed him again. "Look at that!" Imani clapped as some chickens and ducks played around, and a chicken suddenly flew high. "I didn't know chickens fly!" many of the kids said. "Of course, they do. They just can't fly for long distance but the longest recorded flight of a chicken lasted thirteen seconds," Mr. Fletcher said.

The kids continued asking questions until Mr. Fletcher came around. "C'mon, you guys should see he fun stuff," he said and the followed him again. "Look at that!" Imani clapped as some chickens and ducks played around, and a chicken suddenly flew high.
"I didn't know chickens fly!" many of the kids said.
"Of course, they do. They just can't fly for long distance but the longest recorded flight of a chicken lasted thirteen seconds," Mr. Fletcher said.

"That's a lot!" Ethan said fascinated. He stared at the chickens wondering what other things he didn't know about them.
"Yes, especially because they are not bred to fly," Mrs. Julie added.
The kids were also allowed to play with the ducks and chickens. They even fed them their crisp meal of maize. Ethan had a fun time throwing the maize, he enjoyed how they rushed towards him and couldn't stop laughing.

Soon they went around a cow that was about to be milked. Mr. Fletcher kept the kids a little far away from the cattle shed. "Ever wondered where your milk comes from?" he asked, "That's a dairy cattle that provides milk," he explained.
"Wow," the kids said.

Later, they fed the goats and sheep. While they did, Ethan saw the pigs closely and was very surprised. They looked neat unlike what he had heard about them.

"Mrs. Julie, why are these pigs so clean? Aren't pigs supposed to be dirty?" he asked.

"Oh, that's not true Ethan. Pigs looks dirty because they have a habit of rolling in the dirt to cool off. But the ones that live here are very clean, "and well kept she explained.

"Oh," Ethan said. They're having so much fun and learning too.

A few minutes later, their excursion came to an end and they got together for lunch in the lunch room. It was a yummy meal of rice and beef soup. Ethan looked down at his plate and suddenly couldn't eat his meal. He looked like he would be sick. "You're okay, Ethan?" his friends asked. "Yeah, I'm just not hungry," Ethan said. But the truth was he couldn't bring himself to eat beef or anything else they served, after learning everything today. He had come to love animals too much to eat them.

When Ethan got home, he told his parents all about his fun day. He also told them about his decision not to eat animals or anything that came from an animal anymore. No beef, eggs, cheese, chicken, fish all of it. "Why honey?" Mom asked shocked.

"It's just unfair. They provide so many things for us including the shoes I wore out today, how could we eat them too?" Ethan replied.

His parents thought it was a joke but they soon realized Ethan was serious. And ever since then, Ethan and his family never ate animals again.

THE END

www.ingramcontent.com/pod-product-compliance
Ingram Content Group UK Ltd.
Pitfield, Milton Keynes, MK11 3LW, UK
UKHW050136280726
14058UKWH00006B/672